# Light

# on the

# Mountain

### Dr. Stewart Bitkoff

Abandoned Ladder

Printed in the United States of America

ISBN-13: 978-0-9915775-2-1
ISBN-10: 0-9915775-2-3


10  9  8  7  6  5  4  3  2  1

*My thanks to Noah, Jennine, Wendy, Melody, Michael and Leola: all very good team mates.*

## *Better People = A Better World*

*People treat others badly*
*Because they do not know*
*How to treat themselves well.*
*The ills of the world*
*Are correctable only*
*By raising better people.*

*One of the ways*
*Better people are produced*
*Is through human development systems*
*That offer higher knowledge.*
*Higher knowledge is available*
*If you search for it*
*And are fitted to receive it.*
*That is the quandary.*

*The task of the rightly Guided Ones*
*Is to tend the flame of knowledge*
*And under the proper conditions share it.*
*These conditions include:*
*Right time, right place and right people.*

*So you think I am talking in riddles?*
*Perhaps I am or maybe*
*You need to change your way of thinking.*

   *-SB*

# CONTENTS

# THE LEGEND

Among the people of the city plain and mountains
There is an ancient tale
About a magical, glowing Light.
This wonderful Light appears
From time to time
To help people in need
Or those who are frightened
And have lost hope.
In the darkest hour
When all is thought to be lost
This Light appears
And turns problems into solutions.

Over the years countless people have been helped.
The pure of heart, the broken and the lost
Have been rescued
From seemingly impossible situations.
Tradition has it
By focusing inward on the Light
And saying the prayer of submission
Miracles occur.
Further it is believed
That when this Light is about to go out
Another will come to take its place.

Herein is the origin of this Legend.

  *-SB*

# CHARACTERS APPEARING IN STORY

*Ancient One:*    Eternal being and Guardian of the Light.

*Escobar:*    Mountain guide and cousin to Loopi.

*Rosa:*    Wife to Escobar.

*Loopi:*    Young girl of 12 years and cousin to Escobar.

*Rado:*    Youngest member of Council of Governors; former friend of Escobar who is sent to search out second Sun.

*The Guard:*    Company of soldiers joining Rado in his search for second Sun.

*King:*    Distant ruler who demands taxes for War Fund; grandson of former King who banished Priests of Unity.

*Fortuun:*    High Priest (Priests of Unity) leader of the people who prayed for the Ancient One's return.

| | |
|---|---|
| *Mylan, Wylmar:* | Senior members of the Council of Twelve (People of Unity) working with Fortuun. |
| *The People Of Unity:* | Group of 200 believers lead by Fortuun, High Priest who helped pray The Ancient One into existence. |

# THE HOUR OF CHANGE

For millennia the Ancient One slept. Beneath the earth in the subterranean caves of the Oreen Mountains his body waited for the hour of rebirth. Here the temperature preserved the flesh until it was needed again.

During this time of sleep the Ancient One served in other capacities. His soul was of the Anointed and there was work to be done in other forms and worlds. The Light was the binding force which held all things together; he served the Light as few could.

The hour of rebirth was at hand.

———————⊶◆⊷———————

The people were weary from the wars. Long ago tears dried like morning dew on a hot summer's day. Most had forgotten why the wars were fought and lost faith in the Governors. It was the Governors who maintained the wars were necessary.

For the people of the city-plain, it was a time of despair. Elected officials lined their pockets with the peoples' gold and many went hungry. Most of what the people worked to create went to sustain the wars or was lost in graft among the many layers of government.

The people needed change and hope.

---

# DAY ONE

As the morning sun burned away the mountain mist, the Ancient One took his place outside the caves. The mountains were his friends. Until the hour of service they protected and housed him. As he entered into his meditation, and began to reflect the Light across the hills, a wondrous thing happened. Light began to flow from the Ancient One and the mist evaporated. And as this holy man went deeper into his meditation, the Light began to intensify. Slowly he became a sun unto himself.

And as the people of the city-plain looked into the mountains, they saw not one, but two suns. This morning, the eastern sky had two orbs of brilliance to greet the day; one from the heavens and one from the hills beckoning them onward.

And as neighbors called to neighbors to see the miracle in the mountains, their despair began to lift. This day was greeted by a sun of hope.

———————

Escobar beheld the second sun and wondered at its origin. He knew the mountains around the city-plain as well as any. At this point in the eastern slope there was no structure of any kind that might serve as a mirror to reflect the morning sun. All that existed in that location was the entrance to the caves.

Could the caves be leaking a gas that illuminated the slope? That was possible but highly unusual. Escobar continued to stare at the Light. Something seemed to be going on within its energy pattern. Whatever it was, it was calling to Escobar. The energy was pulsating and calling his name.

Escobar the renowned mountain guide stared in amazement. He had never seen anything on the mountains like this and needed to discover its origin.

———————————————

Loopi, a young girl of 12, awoke and looked out her bedroom window. This morning the eastern sky was aglow with two suns. She stared at the horizon transfixed wondering what it meant.

Was the world ending? Or was the world beginning? She was unsure and grew increasingly excited.

As the Ancient One continued his meditation, he could feel the Light reaching the people of the city-plain and knew it had begun.

Like a beacon in the night, the Light was calling to those who were in despair. It was his mission to replace sorrow with joy and anger with love.

And as he continued lighting the morning sky, he lost track of time. He was one with the moment and lost in the glory of the Light.

The Council of Governors arrived. This morning they were to discuss the tax shortfall. Without taxes, they could not meet their portion of the War Fund and the King expected the Governors, personally, to make up the difference. The King allowed the Governors to rule only if the War Fund was maintained. None wished to anger the King or pay with their own gold. The only option was to get the people to work harder. This was the morning agenda.

The four Governors' took their seats and instead of talking of revenues, they discussed the second sun. Everyone including the Governors was bewildered by its origin and significance.

Was this Light permanent? Where did it come from? Should it be investigated? Was it a threat to the city-plain? Did it have economic value?

Throughout the session these questions took precedence over the shortfall in taxes.

---

Then just as unexpectedly as the second sun lit up the morning sky it was gone. One moment, an orb of brilliance and warmth calling to the people of the city-plain, and then it disappeared.

The Ancient One ended his morning meditation. The message was sent. As the Light willed people would respond.

---

For those minutes, when the mountain celebrated its own sun, all the city-plain stopped. Every eye gazed upward toward the mountain. Work halted. People stopped in the fields and factories and began to talk to each other. The despair of the long war years was replaced with a song of hope.

Now the Light was gone and for the people the absence of Light signaled a return to work. For most the second sun was a momentary interlude in a dreary day. As they walked to the factories and fields, the people continued to speak to each other about this wonder. Some claimed it was the result of luminescent cave gas; others said the sun reflected off the coats of a herd of mountain goats. These herds were plentiful and the sun's glare created the brilliant orb. Still others said it was the mountain facing and the sunlight reflected off of the cliffs.

Throughout the day people talked to each other and were caught up in the excitement of the message of hope emitted by the second sun.

---

Since early youth Escobar was a mountain guide. He listened to the others discuss their explanations for the appearance of the second sun. While these were possible, Escobar knew none of them were probable. Something else was going on.

And as Escobar looked around and saw the people excited by the promise raised by this event, he had to see for himself what caused these phenomena. Was this a permanent source of Light and energy? Or was it transitory? Escobar knew the answer was on the mountain and he would find it.

Today the people of the city-plain were filled with hope and anticipation. Temporarily forgotten were the years of war and oppression by the Governors. Again the people were expectant and joyous. If Escobar could find the source of this new Light, might he be able to bring back news that helped people? Intuitively he knew this Light was something good.

If the Light appeared again, in the same location, Escobar wanted to be there. He wanted to examine and learn from it. Escobar asked his wife to quickly prepare food; he had work in the mountains.

For nearly ten years Rosa and Escobar had been married. Rosa was used to her husband leading travelers across the mountains. After all he was a mountain guide. However this morning things were different and Rosa suspected Escobar was going to find the source of the second sun. Although worried she knew none were more qualified.

As Rosa prepared food and got ready to work in the factory, she did not speak of this to Escobar. Rosa realized, that whatever the reason for the appearance of the second sun, their lives would never be the same.

———————————————

Loopi decided she was not going to school. She did not tell this to her parents and went looking for her cousin, Escobar. He was like an older brother and by nature very curious. Loopi knew that he too would want to know more about the mountain sun.

Escobar was considered the best mountain guide. He knew the mountains and their changing conditions. Whenever wealthy caravans had to cross this range his expertise was sought. He studied the weather conditions and the movement of rocks. Escobar had been taught mountain trails and the relationship between plants and animals by his father and grandfather. Over the years Escobar developed an inner feel for the mountains. Loopi was certain Escobar would be able to find the true meaning of the second sun.

———————————————

The Governors were relieved. The people went back to their daily routine. Once the second sun receded people realized there was work to be done and returned to their normal activity. Only minutes were lost from the morning productivity schedule.

Yet as the morning progressed, reports came into the Governors' Chamber that although people were working they were distracted by this morning's event. The second sun was being discussed by everyone and affected the workers' productivity. The morning's quotas for agriculture and manufacturing were not being met.

As the day continued people remained distracted. The Governors realized something must be done. It was decided Rado the youngest Governor would travel to the mountain to discover the phenomena's source. The Governors were worried should it persist, that tax quotas would not be met. If the King's quotas were not met by the people, the money would come out of the Governors' pockets. The King accepted no excuse; money was needed to keep the War Fund going.

Without hesitation Rado accepted the assignment. He viewed this as a sign of recognition by the older, longer tenured Governors. Rado had some knowledge of the mountains, but to insure success a guide and accompaniment of soldiers was needed.

18

Rado was to lead five of the Governors' Guard. This was to assure, if necessary, the new sun's destruction. These troops were known for their determination and ferocity.

Then Rado summoned Escobar.

———— ⬥ ————

Escobar was nearly packed and as he loaded his gear, he heard his cousin Loopi approaching. Escobar turned to greet her. "Loopi it is good to see you, but shouldn't you be in school?" Loopi replied, "Yes, but I have something more important to do." "What is that?" inquired Escobar. "I have to find out about the second sun," said Loopi. "Isn't that what you are preparing to do?"

Escobar smiled and gently replied, "Loopi if your parents allow, I will take you with me." So Escobar kissed Rosa goodbye and they began walking toward Loopi's house.

As the two cousins talked, Escobar was encouraged by Loopi's enthusiasm. It was good to see he was not the only one excited by this morning's event. If others were similarly affected, the second sun might signal an awakening and positive change for the people of the city-plain.

———————◆———————

Escobar was surprised how easily Loopi's parents agreed to the trip into the mountains. They wished they could leave their work in the fields and also join the adventure. When they saw both suns that morning, they realized anything was possible. A glimmer of hope awoke in their hearts.

Both agreed it had been a long time since there was something to be hopeful about. Also Loopi's going made them feel as if they were going. They could live and experience through her adventure.

So the two cousins began their climb. When next the second sun dawned they wanted to be there.

———————◆———————

Rado was annoyed when his guards returned without Escobar. According to Rosa they had just missed him; he left to find the second sun. She informed them that first he was going to stop at Loopi's, which was on the way to the mountain.

Rado mumbled to himself, "The fools should have followed and caught up with him." No matter. As youths Escobar and Rado spent many hours together climbing the mountains. Rado would catch up with his old friend and persuade him to help the Governors. The Governors had to prove that the second sun was natural phenomena. Should it appear daily, without an explanation, the superstitious might attribute a divine origin. In turn this might erode the Governors' control over the people.

The Governors had been in power for nearly 50 years. Years ago the old priests had been driven out by the King. Their religion was dead; it no longer worked for most people. Today what people wanted was gold so they could buy and consume. This was the religion the Governors brought; a stable economy and a job for everyone. In exchange the Governors exacted a percent of each wage. Everyone was guaranteed a job and thus a way to consume. So what if the percent of tax had risen over the years? Who could predict the years of continual war? The aging King had been driven mad by vengeance and greed. Who could have foreseen this?

Originally the Governors started out as businessmen who saw a way to help the people increase profits. Over time they became more powerful. Who could argue with success? Didn't the risk takers deserve to make a profit on their gold?

Hadn't the Governors proved the success of a government built upon economic growth?

Then Rado stopped himself. His mind wandered from the goal. Find Escobar so together they could find the source of the second sun.

This second sun, it had already started to affect the way he worked and thought. It was taking up too much of his time. What of the average worker; how much of their energy was being used up thinking about the second sun?

Rado put on his mountain boots and climbing clothes; then he ordered the Guard to follow. They would join Escobar when he made camp the first night. Rado remembered the spot.

———————————

The Ancient One returned to his body. He traveled to the city-plain in thought-form and saw first hand his effect upon the people. For generations the people suffered. They had given up their freedom in order to worship the God of gold.

'Each had to care for his/her body and the needs of his family, yet material need was only part of a balanced life. Material need was not meant to be the foundation upon which a life was built. Each was a soul that had journeyed to this plane to learn, work and serve. Care of the body and participation in the physical world were only one aspect of the Design. In this age the Governors had made it the design. They entrapped the people through fear; unless they followed the Governors they would go hungry and die. And because the Governors could provide for the peoples' need, the people listened. What began as a means to a complete life became the center of life.

'In part a full life begins with economic stability; yet economics is only one aspect of life. The ancient priests had been replaced by Governors. Although initially well meaning, these positions turned into opportunities through which the people were robbed. Just as the priests sought to control the people through fear so the Governors, in time, did the same. Sadly people sought to become Governors who wished to control instead of serve. One form of corruption was replaced with another.'

Yes. The people needed to be free from their fear. The means to achieve this had just begun.

———————◆◆◆———————

The Priest of Unity waited a long time for this day. With the birth of the second sun, they abandoned their village and were on the road to sit at the Ancient One's feet. Banished to the mountains they lived among the mountain folk for nearly 50 years. Over time they learned to make their living, tending sheep, catching fish and planting.

Now an entire village: men, women, children, dogs and smaller live-stock were on the road heading toward the Light on the Mountain. Since the beginning, this coming had been foretold and they wanted to be present to hear the ancient song of liberation.

Long had they prayed; long had they focused their energy so the Cosmic might again enter the world of forms. Each had suffered and each had feared. Now it was time to end suffering and end fear. The entire village was on the road. Each was sure this was the One who was foretold.

---

Escobar was pleased to have Loopi as a traveling companion. Although she could not keep up with his pace, Loopi did not complain and was excited about the prospect of finding the second sun. She too sensed something wonderful had begun.

For now Loopi and Escobar were free from their everyday activity of school and work. The people of the city-plain had long forgotten there was more to life than the things which could be consumed.

As Escobar looked over his shoulder and saw the city-plain, he realized he was leaving his old life behind. The second sun had given birth to a new part of his life.

———————————

As Rado and his accompaniment of Guards walked toward the mountain and the pass which led to the caves, Rado was reminded of another time: a time when he was free of the responsibility of government and the fear of not meeting the King's tax quota.

That was a very long time ago. In those days all Rado cared about was soaring like the mountain condors that flew higher and higher on the breeze. He too wanted to fly to the very seat of heaven and knock on God's door. For a time, he lived in the mountains like the hermits of old and dedicated his life to climbing and the pursuit of knowledge.

Then Rado went to University and learned there were many Gods and the God which paid the most was the God of gold. Rado joined this religion and quickly rose to the top. Now he was the youngest Governor and one of the high priests of economic stability.

In this religion the rules were very simple. He who made the most gold became the high priest. To maintain this position some of the wealth was shared with the King and people of the city-plain. As long as these two conditions were satisfied, one could remain as high priest, indefinitely. In this position with a little cunning one could keep most of the gold for themselves.

Although imperfect much could be said for this form of government and religion. It served the people; they were content with their jobs and consumer goods. And as Rado continued walking it occurred to him, if this system was so fine and good, why were the Governors concerned about a minor diversion which kept people from working? The second sun distracted people for less than an hour. Surely their form of government could survive this distraction?

Then Rado looked up and saw a condor rising on the mountain breeze and the old longing returned.

———————————◼◆◼———————————

For 50 years Fortuun and his people waited. Years ago when the Priests of Unity were driven out of the city-plain everyone turned to his father the High Priest for leadership. Fortuun the First, lead the people of Unity to a quieter life in the mountains. This was a difficult time. The old ways were gone. Each had to work and contribute to their personal maintenance. The privileged class of Priest and Priestess was abolished. Each had to earn their keep and accepted the mantel of religious service as an additional responsibility.

Now over two hundred strong the people of Unity were going to sit at the feet of the Ancient One. They helped bring that which was formless into the world of forms. It was Fortuun the First who taught, one people working together in harmony, could bring about a miracle.

The Ancient One returned to vanquish fear and relieve suffering. The old was making way for the new; the timeless cycle repeating itself.

———————————————

As the Ancient One sat before the cave, he perceived all that was taking place. He could feel the different forces at work and understood their inevitability. Within each was the capacity to rise higher; this was the center to which he called.

'Willingly he accepted this responsibility and now watched the events unfold. The people of the city-plain were evolving to a higher condition. This was the Plan. As guardian of the Light it was his responsibility to ensure this Plan unfolded accordingly.

'It was an evolution that would take hundreds of years. Yet he had the time to accomplish this for there was no time and space only the Light. The last time he walked few listened. That was a very long time ago. This time, as the Light wills the outcome would be different.

'Yet he could not judge outcomes. His was the role of Guide. That which a person understood and attained was between himself and the Light. He was simply a Messenger. It was a role he accepted since the beginning; when the original pact was made.'

---

As Loopi climbed following Escobar through the pass, she thought of her parents. Both worked from morning until sunset six days a week. This was to pay for all the things they needed. Both toiled in the fields and she wondered why they worked so hard.

One day last week after dinner she asked her father, "You and mother sweat to pay for our food and the things we need, isn't life more than hard work to provide for our body?"

Loopi's father replied. "In each life one has many roles. Sometimes I played the part of athlete and other times the role of son. Now I am provider. So is your mother. My job is to be the best I can at whatever is set before me. Similarly I must never forget the reason for my life. As father, I help guide and love you. I take joy in this and remember the One who gave us this time together."

Was life that simple? Accept each task and do it as well as possible? Loopi realized she had done enough thinking and had better focus her attention on climbing. Escobar was almost out of sight and it was beginning to grow dark. Knowing they would rest soon she picked up her pace.

Twilight came to the mountains and the city-plain and people began to prepare to sleep. When most looked back across their day, they remembered the wonder of the sunrise. Instead of one sun greeting the morning, a second sun joined the morning. Were they not a people blessed? Each had a job, a home and was protected from harm by the Governors. Yet the taxes and endless War Fund were a constant burden. As they reflected, they thought that this was not the time to dwell on politics: it was a time for thankfulness.

---

Rado and his men were tired and decided to rest for the night. They had been unable to catch Escobar. Fortunately this was the safest portion of the climb and they figured to join him by early morning.

Rado watched the sunlight leave the mountains and he remembered how much he missed the quiet and solitude.

---

# DAY TWO

On the distant horizon, the grey thread of dawn appeared. It was that brief time before the sun entered the morning sky. Outside the cave the Ancient One took up his position and began reflecting the Light across the mountains and the city-plain. As they slept, this morning the Light of Eternity preceded the morning sun and caressed everyone.

Slowly people began to awake and prepare for the new day. This day the Light arose not out of the eastern sky where the land met the clouds, but from the slopes of the Oreen Mountains. Today the second sun was first to greet the dawn. Then five minutes later the morning sun joined in the display of Light and two beacons of hope anointed the day.

---

As the people of the city-plain awoke they gazed at the Oreen peaks dazzled by the Light. The colors were a luminescent blue and yellow and filled them with hope. There was no heat emanating from this orb, only layer upon layer of Light, originating from a center of pure blue fire.

On an inner level, the flames seemed to hypnotize and speak to the people. Transfixed each heard the same message. "You have been asleep waiting for this moment. It is here. Drink of the blessings of eternity."

---

By the time the Governors reached their chamber, reports were coming in from all across the city-plain. The people declared a day of celebration. The second sun reminded people they were children of eternity and did not have to toil every day for their bread. The Light would provide. Always there had been enough and they had forgotten to be still and give thanks.

People gathered in neighborhood squares and silently prayed. Others went to visit old friends and many brought presents to the sick. The blue sun kindled a celebration of spiritual love.

The Governors were frightened. It was precisely for this reason their ancestors drove out the priests. People could effectively serve only one master and the Governors wanted them to serve the God of gold, with the Governors as representatives.

———————◆◆◆———————

Loopi woke Escobar and both sat in wonder watching the mountains bathe in the glowing, blue light. Joining in the celebration, eagles and mountain condors circled high above the luminescent peaks.

Then the morning sun joined the celebration of Light. As the sun slowly climbed into the sky, a flock of white doves flew past. Escobar closed his eyes and offered a prayer of thanks.

———————◆◆◆———————

Rado and his men were also awakened by the strange blue Light. Being soldiers their first response was to grab for their weapons. Wondering if they were under attack, they thought the blue Light was a diversion meant to confuse.

But as their eyes adjusted to the blue hue, they realized it emanated from the caves. The same spot as yesterday. Then the morning sun joined in the Light show and Rado's men put down their swords. This was why they were sent; to uncover the source of the second sun.

As Rado watched his men lower their guard, he became even more aware of the power this second sun had upon people. First it bewildered them. Then they were filled with hope. Next they were afraid and finally they accepted it. The second sun was exerting too much influence over the people. This disputed the power of the Governors; they wanted to be the sole power brokers.

Rado ordered his men to be alert and pack up. They had to find Escobar and make their way to the cave of Light. With each hour the situation grew more serious.

------------------

Fortuun finished leading the people of Unity in a short prayer. To everyone this display of Light reinforced why they left their village. Up above on the mountain, the Ancient One waited. Through their prayers the people helped bring the eternal into the world of forms. This was the answer to the darkness which had spread throughout the city-plain. Materialism had choked the life out of Oneness and good. The Ancient One came to provide the antidote.

It was time for a new world and the Ancient One would rekindle the old knowledge. Darkness always preceded the dawn. This was the dawn of a new age. The people of Unity realized this

34

and willingly left behind many of their possessions. Higher up on the mountain, was the Emissary of Light. They had come to join the Light and be one with its brilliance.

After the prayer the people packed and continued their climb upward to the cave.

---

As the Ancient One continued reflecting the Light, he perceived all was in balance. The first to arrive would be those who held firm to the Plan. Next were the pure of heart; they too wished to serve. Following were the detractors and skeptics. And at a distance were the multitudes; in their own way, part of it all.

As it was, so it must be again.

---

And as the sun filled the morning sky the second sun receded. The Ancient One ended his meditation.

Soon the people would arrive. For a time words would replace action. The Ancient One peered out across the city-plain and projected an invitation: "Come we are waiting!"

———————⇒▪◆▪⇐———————

Escobar stopped climbing when he heard the call. Turning, to see if Loopi needed help, Escobar realized the words came from somewhere else.

"Come we are waiting." Who said this? What did it mean? Could it be from the Light on the Mountain? Then Escobar realized it was and he became more excited.

He called to Loopi to quicken the pace.

———————⇒▪◆▪⇐———————

Loopi was trying to keep up with Escobar. When Loopi heard the call, he was 15 yards ahead. Was it her mother? Was she sending a warning? Then Loopi realized the voice came from the blue Light. It was an invitation. The Light was friendly. At the same time, this excited and frightened her.

Continuing up the slope, Escobar called to Loopi, "At this pace we will reach the cave just after lunch." He asked, "Can you continue at this speed?" Loopi called back, "I will do my best."

———————⇒▪◆▪⇐———————

When Fortuun heard the invitation he stopped and realized they were expected. Within the hour the people of Unity would sit at the feet of the miracle maker. The new order had begun; they through their prayers, meditation and faith helped bring it about.

Continuing the ascent Fortuun called to his people. "We are welcome and have been Called to join Him. As you climb the remaining distance leave your worldly thoughts behind. In less than an hour we will be face to face with the Emissary of Light. Prepare yourselves for this glorious hour. Empty yourself of yourself. Soon your higher nature will join the higher destiny of the universe."

———————————

Rado gave up trying to catch Escobar. He could tell from their camp site they were 3-5 hours behind. The remaining climb was the most dangerous and they could not make up the time on that part of the mountain. In fact many had died on this slope and Escobar's experience would have helped make the climb much safer.

From the tracks it appeared that Escobar was not climbing alone. His climbing companion was either a small boy or a woman. What did it matter? They were moving too fast to catch them.

What to do? He had made this climb before but so many years ago. He had to think this through carefully! To turn back now was impossible; failure meant economic death.

———————

Meanwhile hundreds of miles away in the Northern Province, the King was being briefed by one of his advisors.

He wondered, "Could it be true? The Light on the Mountain . . ." The message sent by carrier pigeon was short. He would wait for other messages and more details. The King excused himself from court and the business of running the country. He had to think and recall what his grandfather said. It was grandfather who chased away the Priests of Unity and spoke of future events.

———————

The Governors lost control at that point and they knew it. The day turned into a festival. The people of the city-plain were singing, dancing and sharing their goods with each other. Few went to work.

Some said it was the end of the world. Others claimed it was the beginning of a new age. The Governors were frightened and ordered their Guard to go on alert. They hoped, as the Light on the Mountain faded, so would the peoples' joy and everyone would return to normal activity and keep working.

At this point to confront the people and force everyone to return to work would be a mistake. The people had to work in order to eat; everyone knew this. If provoked the Governors feared the people would recognize them as the real source of their problems; revolt and take back what was rightfully theirs.

Also the Governors knew soon the King would learn of this either through his spies or simply by noticing the loss of revenue. By each hour the situation became more serious. The Governors sent a dispatch to Rado, "Events are growing worse. Quickly find the Light and extinguish." The fastest climber in the Guard carried this message.

It was mid-morning when the people of Unity arrived. They assembled 40 yards below the ledge upon which the Ancient One rested. Without a word, each sat in place, closed their eyes and focused inward on the Light.

Each man, woman and child was still, drinking in the Light of Eternity. Not a word was spoken; each knew and was filled. This was the hour of prayer. This was the moment of grace.

———————————◆◆◆◆◆———————————

Escobar and Loopi continued to climb upward. Loopi was growing tired and called to Escobar to rest. They had been moving at a fast pace for hours.

As the cousins knelt beneath the shade of a large rock Loopi inquired, "Did you feel it? As we climbed I felt some kind of energy enter my body. It was uplifting and kind. Telling me everything would work out. We are doing the right thing."

Escobar replied, "I too felt it. It was like morning when the second sun appeared. I thought I was home again; a little boy in my mother's arms."

Inwardly Escobar wondered what they would find on the mountain. He figured they would reach their destination, as planned, by early afternoon. He put his concerns aside and motioned to Loopi to continue their ascent.

———————————◦◦◦◦◦◦———————————

After the silent prayer the people of Unity set about the task of making camp. They put up their animal skin huts; scouts were sent to find water; hunters went looking for game; children began to play in open spaces; and mothers began to bake.

Fortuun gathered together the Council of Twelve and the Ancient One withdrew to his cave. The purpose of the Council's meeting was to create a plan to approach the Ancient One and establish rules of conduct for the people. None knew how long they would be on the mountain or how long their encounter with the Ancient One would last.

Fortuun was first to speak. "That which we have prayed for has come to pass. We are within yards of the Ancient One and none knows how to approach that which is most holy. We are like school children too shy to approach our teacher. I will take suggestions."

Mylan one of the eldest spoke. "We have set up camp at a distance due to respect and reverence. This morning's prayer was proof that our actions to date have been accepted. Each tasted of the Light and received the answer for which they prayed. As God Wills, the Ancient One will signal how and when we are to approach."

Wylmar another elder added, "I agree with Mylan. We need not make this a very complicated matter. According to Prophecy the Ancient One has awakened. We are here as servants and witnesses to this miraculous event. When it is time, we will receive the teaching. Until then our duty is to maintain a normal life. We have responsibilities to our families and the young.

"My suggestion is to maintain normal routine and take time each day to say the silent prayer. After performing our daily work, we as a people should come together and turn inward toward the Ancient One. He will signal when to approach."

Unanimously the Council of Twelve agreed to this plan.

---

Inside the cave the Ancient One turned inward and drank of the timeless Light. He gazed back into the past and far, far ahead into eternity. He saw himself as a link in a chain which reached into pre-history and into the evolving future.

'Humanity was moving toward a higher condition. It was his duty to assist in this evolution. He took a physical form so the message might be sent. He became one of them so he could lead and serve.

The message was the same; it was always the same. Yet the garment it wore was different. These were mountain people and the garment must be able to withstand both the hot and cold of the upper ranges.

'Once he too had a life and family. But that was many, many years ago before the Light alchemized his soul.

'The message to be delivered originated in another dimension. He was merely the voice. In time the message would be forgotten and he or another would come to remind them.'

———————————

Rado and his accompaniment of soldiers continued to climb. They left behind their swords, shields and armor. In order to reduce the risk of falling, they kept only the clothing they wore and daggers. It had been years since Rado lead a climb on this face of the mountain. Each knew the lighter the load, the better the balance and quicker the reaction time.

Upward they climbed unsure if any would leave the mountain alive.

———————————

The people of the city-plain lived this way as long as anyone could remember. Years ago they left their mountain villages and began to work for others.

In the beginning this way of life was very appealing; hunger was eliminated. The large farm and factory work provided enough jobs and food to live stress-free lives. As commerce grew there was a need for an army to protect the traders. Then an alliance with the King was formed. Except for the tax on goods, the King allowed the city-plain to grow without control. Over the years as more goods were traded taxes increased. Somehow gold was always plentiful.

So for many years, in contrast to the harshness of the mountains, this was an easier life. In the mountains one had to hunt for food and success was dependent on weather conditions. Winter in the mountains could be very harsh.

It was decades before the people realized they traded their personal freedom for false stability; economic growth could not continue forever. Few understood the resources of the city-plain were finite.

Over the years key materials began to shrink. Water had to be transported from the mountains through an aqueduct system. This was a costly process. Also farm land became less productive and farmers had to work harder. All the while taxes increased and people became fearful of not meeting the tax quota.

For the average citizen this was a difficult time. Could they retain their jobs and continue to raise their families? As they grew more dependent upon others for manufactured goods, the hours of labor increased and the inner life was gradually forgotten.

---

When the King banished the Priests to the mountains, the death of the city-plain was sealed. All civilizations exist for a time, then, evolve into something else. This is the way of all things. This banishment was one of the final events.

Even if the Priests had been allowed to hold power other forces were at work which made the collapse inevitable. The balance had long shifted. The people became too reliant upon others, lost their independence, and had forgotten to develop their higher nature.

The Priests became greedy and wanted more power. Their leaders were organizing to take control away from the King. When the King uncovered this plot, he executed the leaders and banished the remaining Priests. Fortuun the First was leader of this exiled group who made their new home in the mountains.

Over time artists and other free-minded citizens joined this community. The rule of the Governors and their tax quota was not for everyone. And as the people of Unity relearned the ways of living in the mountains, there was a rebirth of the Old Faith. This religion sang the song of the Ancient One who was reborn every 1000 years to rekindle the fire of worship and could reappear any time he was needed. Various legends described a high being that slept in the mountains and appeared when people were in trouble. One tale told the story of an old shepherd who saved little children from harm when they wandered away from their families. Another tale spoke of a kind stranger who appeared at the hut of an old mountain couple to heal their fevers. These and other legends celebrated the Ancient One's capacity to appear any time and help people. This was in addition to his 1000 year mission.

In time the people of Unity began to pray, daily, for the Ancient One to return and make their world a better place. Some prayed because they wanted what had been taken; others prayed for a world of spiritual peace and brotherhood.

What the people wanted had come to pass. The Cosmic reasons for this incarnation were known only by the Ancient One and the Light.

———————

Lovingly, the King thought about his grandfather. His own father died when he was a boy and his grandfather raised him. While King, his grandfather secretly held to the Old Faith and schooled his grandson in the ways of the mountains.

Grandfather often wished he would be alive when the Light on the Mountain next appeared. In their quiet talks he shared this with his grandson.

When grandfather banished the Priests to the mountains he knew this was according to Plan. Also he made sure his grandson understood the importance of assisting when next the Light appeared. He taught the boy, "People without faith were a people without heart and people without heart could not endure."

———————⟫◆⟪———————

As morning became afternoon, Loopi and Escobar arrived on the mountain. They saw before them a small village of animal skin huts. They walked into the village, to get a closer look at the ledge and cave above. Then Fortuun called out, "Welcome strangers to our camp. I see you also have been called by the Light."

Escobar replied, "We could not stay away. Tell us what you have found?"

Then Fortuun invited Loopi and Escobar into his hut. After some refreshment Fortuun told them what he knew.

———————⟫◆⟪———————

It was just before dusk and the sun was beginning to set. All the people of Unity gathered to sit before the Ancient One. They were arranged, at a distance, just below the ledge on which the Ancient One prayed.

After the silent prayer the Ancient One spoke.

"I have come to renew your religion. It has grown old and tired. I am the water of life and beckon you to join the Light. Come move closer to me."

48

Together all the people moved closer to the Ancient One.

"Because some have come who cannot communicate through spirit, on their behalf and for the others who follow, I will use words. Yet the message is conveyed not by words, but through spiritual energy, Light and love."

———————————◆———————————

It was dusk when Rado and his soldiers reached the mountain crest. They saw hundreds of people, looking upward at the ledge and the Ancient One. All eyes were focused on him.

Strangely enough, Rado thought he saw a ring of Light about the old one's head. This Light joined the dozens of camp fires which were aglow on the mountain. Rado told his men to be still and move in closer to hear what was being said.

———————————◆———————————

As the Ancient One spoke, the sun fell further behind the mountain yet the mountain was aglow with Light.

Filled with wonder, the people of the city-plain looked up and saw the mountain again resplendent with Light.

"This is a dark age. Many have lost hope and are crippled with fear.

"Many years ago, I too walked among you and felt the burdens of the flesh. Through the mercy of the Light I have been freed of pain, suffering and fear. What I offer you has always been available. Never was there a time when it was not there for you. The Light is most merciful and beckons each person. Here take this opportunity and join with me as we celebrate the dawn of a new age. The elements of right time, right place and right people have combined and this is a special hour.

"The people of the city-plain are bound by fear and the oppression of others. In order to live a complete life, a life that is free of the chains which bind each person and hold them back, each must enter on the path to completion. This is a spiritual path; a path which combines the needs of the body with the needs of the spirit. This is the only way to be free. By submitting to our higher nature and the higher destiny of the universe; we are free in the Light.

"Each is a soul and chooses to take on a body and enter the physical realm. This realm is a place where great spiritual progress can occur. Here the soul must choose to rise higher than the physical reality. Because the physical world pulls at the body, there are many distractions and those who choose the Light rise higher than angels.

"Over the next days I will answer questions. I know what is in your heart because I am one of you. The Light has chosen me to return and reveal those things which are needed so all might benefit. As the sun greets the morning and shares the Light with all creatures so this message is for everyone. Record it in your books and in your hearts.

Now let us close our eyes in prayer and tomorrow morning we shall begin anew."

After the silent prayer slowly people began to return to their huts. It was at this point Rado left his men and began to search for Escobar. Rado hoped to discover what had occurred prior to his arrival.

In time Rado was taken to Fortuun's hut. Rado requested food for his men and joined Escobar and Loopi who were also seated inside.

Gradually Rado was able to learn this encampment had just been formed. The people of Unity arrived this morning. To them the Light on the Mountain represented years of prayer and waiting. This was the Deliverer who the people prayed would lead them out of the darkness and restore the Old Faith.

51

Escobar and Loopi felt an undeniable pull to the mountain. There was no other way for them to describe it. Yes they had been curious about the second sun, just as the others, but there was something more. They had to come and see for themselves.

So far all that had happened were moments of silent prayer and an opening statement which Rado heard.

Rado thought if the Ancient One had designs of power or was insane it was too early to tell. While their religion recognized the potential of rebirth and the cyclic appearance of Great Souls, Rado was unsure what he was dealing with.

Rado sat in Fortuun's hut beside Escobar and Loopi and saw the joy on their faces. Intuitively Rado knew his world was changing. He could not get the picture of the Ancient One, bedazzled by Light, out of his mind. The movement of Light about the Ancient One, was it a reflection from the campfires or was something else going on?

---

During the night the King slipped away from the Royal City. Traveling only with the Captain of the Guard they headed toward the city-plain.

Governance would continue under the Queen's direction; in some ways she was more able than he. The Queen had patience and a talent for politics. He fulfilled his responsibilities because he was raised to do so yet he often relied upon her judgment.

The two traveled through the night toward the mountain and city-plain, and the King was filled with excitement about what he would find. He knew the old way of governing, through fear, would be replaced by something higher and he was unafraid.

———————————

That evening most of the city-plain slept. There was a peace and sense of hope in the air. Most went to bed anticipating the dawn. Were they not the people of two suns? Were they not blessed?

Only the Governors and their messenger did not sleep. The Governors feared they lost the people and plotted how they might regain control. The messenger climbed slowly and carefully through the night. He was promised a great reward if he brought the Governors' message to Rado before the next sunset.

———————◗▶◆◀◖———————

The Ancient One rested in the cave while his soul joined the Light: dancing across creation.

———————◗▶◆◀◖———————

# DAY THREE

When morning came to the city-plain, again, two suns awoke to greet the day. The people of the city-plain, as they began their morning routine, were caressed by the Light of two celestial orbs. This filled them with joy and excitement.

On the ledge, the Ancient One reflected the Light of Eternity to the mountain peaks, the nearby huts and country side; on this Light sang his message of hope.

"Know each is born into this world so they can reach higher. Here there is an opportunity to advance. Each is a soul who must travel through the many worlds to find completion. In this realm the journey may be accomplished in an instant. Accept the Light and make your life an hour of service. In this service you shall find your essential oneness with all creation.

"It is your fear which prevents you from becoming one with your lasting self. This fear resides in that part of the soul which is tied to the earth. This part questions and wants to know why? The higher or lasting self provides the answer. In order to listen to this part of your soul, you must temporarily turn away from your worldly self.

"That part which is tied to the physical is necessary so the soul might function in this world. Similarly it must be put aside so the higher nature might emerge. This nature is transcendent and integrates both aspects of the soul.

"All manner of illness and fear are created, if the soul relies too heavily on the worldly or cognitive portion. Many believe all problems can be solved by intellect and reason. This is not so. Some problems are spiritual in nature and can only be solved when the soul learns to center itself on the Light.

"As this capacity to experience the Light matures so the soul is able to rise beyond its fear of death. For as the intellect stands aside or momentarily dies so the higher nature emerges.

"This morning the sun of the eastern sky represents our worldly need. Similarly the Light on my heart represents the Light within each soul. Both Lights are necessary for the soul's journey through this world. Both capacities are necessary for the task of completion."

By this time many had moved closer to the Ancient One. Like a moth to a flame they drew closer to experience more of themselves. Then a young shepherd stood and called out. "O holy one how should we spend our lives? Are we to give up the life of this world for the life of the spirit? Surely this is the lasting life!"

The Ancient One smiled and replied. "If all turned to the Light, at the expense of the world, who would tend the flocks? Who would gather the wool for our garments and raise the animals for our food? In all things it is a matter of balance and attitude. If the task is done for the Light because you are a servant of the Light, then, it is a prayer which will carry you into the next world."

Next Loopi stood and called out. "Your words frighten me; you speak of fear and the life which is lasting. All I know is what I see and feel. Why should I believe you and seek something I cannot see?"

Again the Ancient One spoke. "Little one in the quiet of the evening and in your mother's caress you can perceive the Light. This capacity to understand where you came from and where you are going is as natural as the hunger in your belly.

"Within each there is the capacity to be one with the Light. Its call can be heard in the quiet of your soul. This capacity sings when it sees the sunrise and celebrates in the robin's flight.

"What I give you are the tools to begin the journey and the grace of the path. The ability to travel the path is within each of you. It is your birthright and destiny."

Fortuun stood and questioned. "Do you advise we turn from the religion of our birth? Was this not a true path helping lead our ancestors closer to the truth?"

"I have not come to tear down what was built before me. I have come to update it. For its time the Faith of your fathers served them. This is another time. The conditions are not the same. The universe, this world and your soul are forever evolving, spiraling upward. What I give is the path for today. It has always been and will always be. Yet for this time and place, as you accept it, it is the path for now."

Rado was next to speak, "Ancient One, forgive me, but I hear no path in your words. All I hear is philosophy and fine words. Where are the instructions and exercises?"

"He who is master teaches by his being. In every breath and deed there is a lesson. My words travel on energy; this energy is the Light of the Universe. It is the binding and creative force. In order for a life to be complete, the life must be aligned with this energy. This is accomplished by saying the prayer of submission. Each path has a version of this prayer.

"For now the prayer is as follows. Say it morning and evening or as many times as you wish. These words attune you to the Infinite.

> *O Lord, I surrender myself to You.*
> *It is from You I came*
> *And it is back to You I am going.*
> *Guide me through this day.*
> *O Lord, I open myself to my higher nature*
> *And the higher destiny of the universe.*
> *O Lord, guide me through my life.*

"As you say each word, focus on it and its meaning. See the Light in each word. Gradually by repeating this prayer morning and evening, as the Light wills, your life will come into balance with the higher destiny of the universe.

"Now let us say this prayer together. Repeat the words slowly, then, close your eyes and focus on the Light."

And as each person repeated the prayer of submission and focused inward, their soul joined with the Light and they experienced their transcendent selves.

It was mid-morning and Rado was sitting by himself, looking out across the city-plain. Everything he knew and thought about was challenged by the Ancient One. In just a few minutes the focus of his life shifted.

It was not the Ancient One's words which disturbed him, he had heard these promises before; it was the experience of the Light. After saying the prayer, which he really did not believe, suddenly, something happened. He was taken to another part of himself. He felt connected to all things. He became part of the soldiers, the people on the mountain and the Ancient One. Next he joined the mountain condor and flew upward toward the sun. As he flew higher and higher, he sang a song of freedom, celebrating his immortality and kinship with the Light. Then he found himself back in his body.

Everyone else had left. He was alone seated before the Ancient One. The Ancient One opened his eyes, looked into Rado's soul and smiled, offering, "So you wanted to be free like the condor." Then the Ancient One disappeared.

Now Rado felt empty and worried. Had he spent his life seeking the wrong things? What should he do? With his powers was the Ancient

One a threat? Then Rado realized he was giving into his fear; he was spending too much time with the every day, cognitive portion of his consciousness. He was thinking, not simply being.

Slowly he began to repeat the prayer of submission. After a time he was again at peace.

———————————

The Ancient One sat in the darkness of the cave and reflected the Light of Eternity to the people on the mountain and city-plain. His heart was the mirror upon which the Eternal Light reflected and all were invited to celebrate their immortality.

———————————

# DAY FOUR

Just before dawn the King awoke and turned inward focusing his gaze on the mountain. Gradually he felt the Ancient One and although miles away was one with the new sun.

———————◄►◄►————————

At their early morning conference the Governors were frantic. It was evident they had lost control of the people. Many refused to pay their daily tax or report to work.

A report prepared by the Bureau of Monitoring stated the following:

> Many of the people claim they are free. They say the new sun has heralded the beginning of a golden age and the Governors cannot force them to work. They claim the Governors no longer have the power. The people of the city-plain outnumber the Governors' troops 20 to 1; if the Governors persist in their demands they will be killed.

The people realize there is no profit in death. Dead workers cannot produce and the Governors risk death if they oppose the people. The new sun heralds the beginning of a spiritual age; the physical world has long pulled them in the wrong direction. Further the people feel in time, new leaders will emerge who will lead them into a world which balances both the physical and spiritual.

---

Morning on the mountain brought a light steady rain. The land was dry and quickly drank the liquid of life. As Rado watched the falling drops he saw someone approaching. From a distance, it was difficult to identify the traveler, but the colors were unmistakable. The purple and white breastplate with the Governors' crest was unmistakable.

Rado stepped out into the rain and signaled the messenger. He stumbled forward, handing Rado a sealed message. The seal was intact and Rado knew he was first to read the contents. "Events are worse. Find the Light and extinguish." So the Governors wanted the Ancient One killed. Rado hesitated to think about this particularly after yesterday's experience.

Rado signaled his men to assist the messenger into the hut. The messenger was to be given whatever refreshment he needed.

<hr />

It had been years since Rado and Escobar spoke to each other. As youths they climbed the mountains and shared similar dreams. Escobar was first to marry and join the work force. Later Rado went off to University and prepared for a life in government. He wanted to be one of those who gave the orders and determine what others did.

The rain stopped and the sun was coming out from behind the clouds. Now as the two old friends sat around the fire it was as if no time had passed. They had been like brothers. Rado broke the silence. "Escobar what do you make of all this? Is this real or some kind of trick?" Then Loopi awoke and sat beside her cousin. Before answering Rado's question, Escobar smiled at Loopi.

"Something strong and deep within pulled Loopi and me to this mountain. We saw the two suns and their effect upon the people, but something else made us come. If we did not make the climb we knew we would remain incomplete."

Rado turned to Loopi for clarification. "Yes. I asked my cousin if I could come. I did not know what was on the mountain but I had to be here. My parents sent me with their blessing. Usually I am not a person to do things without thinking them out but this was just something I had to do."

Next Escobar asked Rado what he thought of the Ancient One's message and the phenomena of Light.

Rado replied, "I will always be grateful the Governors chose me to come. What is going on here will be recorded for many years. As a child of the universe, I am amazed at what I have seen and heard. In my official capacity as one of the Governors, I am confused about what to do."

Then Escobar wondered out loud, "Why do you have to do anything?"

"Because it is my duty!" exclaimed Rado.

"From confusion comes order. In time I am sure you will know what to do," said Escobar.

Rado thought to himself how can I kill this wonderful old man? That is what the Governors want.

66

Loopi called out, "Cousin I am hungry! Let's get breakfast." Escobar called to Rado, "Come join us while we catch some mountain trout."

Then Rado got up and left his official duties so he could join an old friend and his cousin fish for breakfast.

---

After the morning prayer the people of Unity looked up at the Ancient One and waited for his message. The old one began. "Within each there is capacity both to destroy and create. This duality mirrors the cosmic potential. Yet capacity for good and positive work exceeds the negative, tenfold. The Light is all good however the darkness exists for a purpose. One could not be without the other. Remember he who created both Light and darkness is greater than both."

Then a cloud moved in front of the sun and the people felt a cool breeze across their backs. Falling into the shadows, an old woman screamed and another called out, "Are you an evil magician? How can both the sunlight and darkness be equal? Good always triumphs over evil. Let the sunlight return!"

With this challenge the people of Unity were growing frightened and wanted an answer to the charge of magic. The Ancient One stood, opened his arms, and the clouds separated to emit the sunlight. This brought a great cheer from the people. When the noise subsided the old one continued.

"What you have just seen is nothing more than natural phenomena. The clouds obscured the sun and the wind blew them away. This you attribute to me but I am not the cause. He/She who created the Light and its companion the darkness is greater than both. He is the Causer and may be perceived in the energy which surrounds my words. The Light is phenomena. The darkness is phenomena. Go beyond both to the Causer. Herein is Truth. I give you Light because you need Light to believe. Yet the darkness exists for its purpose. In the darkness you rest and draw closer to those you love. You huddle about the fire, look up at the stars and wonder about the purpose of life.

"In the darkness all manner of creatures scurry about the mountain; they help to keep the balance on the slope. What would the mountain be without the bat, the owl or the night crawler? It is the same in the world of spirit. Each creature has to bow before the Truth."

Then Wylmar stood and called out. "Why do you give us a metaphysical doctrine about darkness and Light? The city-plain is being destroyed by greed. Our sons die in battle far away, leaving behind our widowed daughters. The priests have been driven out and the people have no religion. Our Governors burden us with taxes to support a distant King. The people call out for hope and salvation. All you give us is metaphysics and abstract ideas that have no proof in our day to day lives!'

This outburst silenced the crowd. Many were ashamed and others frightened. Would the Ancient One be offended and still the sun forever?

Gently the old one replied, "Does not the sun always follow the night? Does not the spring always follow the winter? Both are expressions of the Light or Truth. In this realm both exist for a purpose and call the traveler toward Truth.

"Yes. The balance has been disturbed. That is why I have come to apply the corrective. The corrective is individual citizens who understand why they are born, and why they have to die and what they are to do with the hours between. Better people who seek the highest potential in themselves and in every action make a better world.

"This life is to be an hour of service; helping self and others reach higher. This service will be understood, as the individual says the prayer of submission and seeks to live a complete life aligned with Truth."

Then the Ancient One sat down, closed his eyes and began to reflect the Light out across the city-plain. The intensity of the Light became so strong it drove the people of Unity back into their huts.

———————

It was late afternoon, again, the people of Unity gathered to hear the Ancient One's message. Some called him Redeemer others an old fool. Yet all agreed this was no ordinary man and what they were seeing would forever change the city-plain. Word had traveled to the mountain, the people of the city-plain refused to work. Many were climbing the mountain to see the messenger for themselves.

Long ago Fortuun and his people established a carrier pigeon system and received daily messages from the city-plain. The Council of Twelve was pleased but also very nervous. Their prayers had been answered yet to what effect? Where would this lead? In the past civil unrest led to bloodshed; everyone hoped this would not be repeated.

———————◆◆◆◆◆————————

Now it was again time to hear the Ancient One's message. He had taken his seat on the ledge and the people of Unity grew silent.

"The ultimate purpose for each life is to grow closer to Truth. Each soul chooses life and death to journey ever upward toward the Light. This is our ultimate purpose. While in this realm there are many things to experience. Each soul's task is to make their life an hour of joy and service. Each is created with wondrous talent, opportunity and choice. The life that is in harmony is the life that is centered on Truth. Remember better people make a better world.

"The higher perception or soul's capacity to experience the Light is the rider on the horse. Your soul knows the direction and how to make the journey. Yet the horse or body must be fed and maintained. The journey is one of Light, joy, wonder and love."

Then a young girl stood and called out, "Kind sir I wish to be a musician, how do your words apply to me? If I am busy centering myself on the Light how will I practice my notes and lessons?"

"Little one you wish to make beautiful songs because that is your nature. Yes, you must practice and work hard. Similarly you must focus yourself upon the Light. Here you center yourself and bring vibrancy and energy to your other talents. In this matter it is not a question of one or another. You have many capacities; each is a gift. In order for them to grow and flower, they must be given expression. You must work at them; but the centering force, for the most good and greatest capacity, is the Light. Sing your songs. Make wondrous music and make it as a servant of the Light."

Then the little girl's mother stood and questioned. "I have always wanted my daughter to raise a family. She wishes to be a musician. You tell her to seek the Light. I am confused. In my time we had no such choices. With all due respect, old one, how can one be so many things?"

"Do not limit yourself. You are created with many talents. Each is an expression of the limitless nature of the universe. Who says you cannot be these things and more? Who told you this?

"My children this was a story you told yourselves. You learned this from one another.

"I tell you, you can be more than you ever dreamed. Each is a limitless potential. This potential finds expression and matures when you are in harmony with the Light. You grow in harmony with the Light, initially, by saying the prayer of submission. This prayer works as a homing device. Just as you have taught birds to find their way home with messages so the Light works in a similar way. Light is attracted to itself.

"The Light is all around and inside you. It is a nutrient, a life giving force, helping you to grow and expand. By saying the prayer of submission, your higher nature tunes to the Light. This inner capacity calls to the Light which is most like itself. Within each person there are many capacities. Do not limit yourself by saying I can only do this or that. You have a hundred different abilities."

Then an old man stood and spoke. "Ancient One I fear that I have reached the end. I can feel my body growing tired. What waits on the other side? I am frightened and need comforting."

"This is a time of answering questions. The secrets of both worlds are to be revealed. This is my duty. Yet you must remember the capacity to answer this question is also within you. The point of this life, in part, is to prepare you for the next world and the world after that.

"This realm is only one among the many that await you. In each you are to experience yourself and the Light: serve and love. The Light loves you. Remember if you take one step toward the Light, the Light will take ten steps toward you.

"Where were you before you were born? What was your experience before you entered your mother's womb? This spark of energy you call life, where was this spark before it took a physical form?

"My friend you are an eternal child of the universe. You had existence before entering this world and will have existence after you leave. While in this realm you are to grow in harmony with the Light. In this service you will find the answer to your questions.

"Do not fear. When you make the transition to the other side, I will be there to help you."

Then Rado stood and asked the question he had been sent to ask. As the confrontation began everyone held their breath.

"Ancient One, here on the city-plain, the people serve the Governors who in turn report to the King. You are calling everyone to serve the Light. How does one person serve two masters?"

"The question you have asked has both a simple and complex answer. Its ultimate answer has already been given. Let me repeat it for you and the others who may need clarification.

"Within each there are many capacities or abilities. If a child wishes to be a musician, she must follow or serve her music teacher. Similarly if she wishes to be a good wife she must serve or work for her family.

"The point of offering a system of spiritual development is to present a path by which people can develop all potentials and strive for excellence. One of these potentials is to be good citizens and work for the benefit of all.

"The problem with most people and this includes governments is they have lost sight of the importance of multi-level development. When the goal is a complete person, someone who thinks of themselves and others, you have good governments. When selfish people gain control, using the government for their own purpose, problems arise. Public servants must serve the public not themselves. Who does the King serve? Who do the Governors serve?

"People must follow rules and laws. But who are the laws set up to protect and help? If they are established for the Governors and Kings, instead of the people, they are bad laws.

"I am not a politician or a Governor. I am a servant of the Light. My job is to help make complete people who can become Governors. A complete person, who is aligned with Truth, makes good decisions that benefit everyone and reaches toward excellence.

"It is possible to serve many masters however ultimately we must serve our own higher nature and the higher destiny of the universe.

"Taking the food out of a hungry child's mouth, to line your own pocket, how does a government call this service? By sending husbands and sons off to fight wars in distant lands so the makers of armaments might grow richer, how is this service to the higher good?

"Yes, some wars must be fought. Laws must be upheld and taxes gathered. If all these things were done in submission to the Light and the higher destiny this would be a wondrous thing.

"Each time you are worried about a decision, ask yourself, will this action bring me closer to my higher self and the higher destiny of the universe? What if each session of government, each war and each meal began with the prayer of submission? Help me O Lord to be in alignment with my higher self and the higher destiny of the universe. In time wouldn't this be a better world?"

Feeling rebuked by the Ancient One's words Rado pressed for clarification. "Here we have separated functions of religion and government. In our mind these two things are different. How can mere words or a prayer make things better?"

The Ancient One smiled. "You ask very good questions, but they come from your mind not your heart and soul. The problem is that you have separated the parts of yourself. You have not unified all your capacities and have excluded an essential aspect. All capacities must be used.

"Does not a King or Governor have a higher nature? Is there not a part of each that is bound to the Light? This part must be awakened and used so that each will be at their best when serving others. I do not tell you to exclude your intellect and understanding of governmental law in making decisions. The problem is that you have not used your higher capacity. I tell you learn to govern yourself. When you govern yourself you will be a better governor who serves the people.

"Of course mere words or prayers cannot change things. People change things. If words are said without the proper focus they are meaningless. If a prayer is said without sincerity and not aligned with the Light it is an empty prayer.

Similarly if promises are made to individuals or people without the intent of their being met, they are empty and manipulations.

"Better people make better leaders. Better leaders make better government. This we can all agree upon.

"Now it is time for us to rest and end for the day. Let us close our eyes and pray together; in silence we will use this opportunity to reach higher."

Then most of the people turned inward and repeated the prayer of submission.

---

As twilight came to the country-side, the King gazed out at the distant mountains. At the base of this range lay the city-plain. He was aware of the civil disorder but he wanted to see the Light for himself. Within a large kingdom there was always a sector that was in unrest. Restoring order could wait. However, the Light on the mountain- that was a once in a lifetime experience.

Knowing its significance and cause the King wished to by-pass the city-plain and go directly to the mountain. While it was his duty to correct the unrest he wanted to experience the Light.

After the King said his prayer and entered into meditation he changed his mind. During his meditation the King saw an old man who was seated. And as the King, with his inner eye beheld the Ancient One, they spoke mind to mind.

*"Go fulfill your duty. Leave this mountain to the Light.*

*Fulfill your duty. In the city-plain you have work to do."*

In the morning the King and his Captain headed toward the city-plain to restore order. The King planned to replace the Governors with an honest ruler: himself. The people were now ready for such a government; the missing ingredient had been added.

---

Fortuun and Rado sat outside Rado's hut. It was Fortuun who began. "So what are you going to do? You did not come to the mountain only to hear the Ancient One's words. You were sent for something else. The soldiers and messenger indicate this."

Rado looked at Fortuun and realized he could kill Fortuun in a moment; as a Governor Rado had the authority. Yet this second sun and what it meant was more important than the commitments of their individual lives.

Rado began. "I have been sent to extinguish the Light. The city-plain is in chaos and the Governors voted for death."

Fortuun stared at Rado and replied. "We would not let you do that. We have waited too long."

"You could not stop me. Including myself we are seven trained soldiers against shepherds, women and children."

"We are prepared to die to save the Ancient One."

Rado smiled and replied. "That will not be necessary. In the morning I will send my men off the mountain. I wish to join you and serve the Ancient One. He has touched a part of me that I had forgotten. When the Governors learn I have joined you, it is possible they will come after us both. What do you say to that?"

"Then that is the way it must be. This hour has been prophesized. It is our duty to protect and allow what is to be."

Then Fortuun and Rado closed their eyes and embraced the Light, submitting to the higher destiny of the universe.

The Ancient One, deep in meditation, realized his time on the mountain was coming to an end. The pieces of the plan had come together. He was the corrective. Hope replaced fear. Goodness replaced greed and the people had an updated code by which they could live.

In time when the people forgot and strayed, another would come to remind them.

Humanity was evolving to a higher condition. By following the path, what an individual soul could accomplish in a life-time, humanity would accomplish over the next four hundred years.

No one could say if this was right or wrong; it was simply the higher destiny of the universe.

# DAY FIVE

---

It was the morning of the fifth day and the Ancient One called everyone to him. Seated on the ledge, 20 feet above the people of Unity, he went into his meditation. As he reflected the Light across the mountain and the city-plain, he spoke out and hearts aligned themselves with his eternal message.

"In the years to come many will glorify my words and actions. They will debate about what was intended and what was not. They will examine my effect to determine if it was miraculous. Remember the message is not my words or their effect. They are a small part. The message is the energy which enables and is the Ultimate Reality. This Light is the mother and father of us all.

"In this time of my coming people were blocked by fear and conditioning. This fear kept them from going further, examining and becoming what was intended. Together we have learned to close our eyes to the every-day self for a time, each day, and listen to that part which is eternal. It is not the part which is afraid: it is the part which knows the truth.

"This is the spiritual consciousness and may be awakened by saying the prayer and trying to live a life of service. The life of service is the complete life. Before this awakened life can be attained other things must be left behind.

"Leave behind your preconceptions about yourselves. Each is blocked by thought patterns which are based upon the current social reality. Enlightenment cannot be attained only by thinking things out or discussing things; it is attained through perception of Reality. The part of the consciousness which is adept at perceiving is awakened by saying the prayer of submission. This prayer tunes the consciousness to this Reality. Your present ideas about your life, your religion and relationships must be put aside daily for a time. Then you might experience lasting Truth. When you have learned to experience this Reality; you know the goal and are ready to travel alone.

"Chief among fear and preconception is the fear of death. Yet the physical body must die: that is its destiny. Why do you fear something which is natural? You fear it, because it is our very nature to fear what is unknown and potentially painful. Yet with the pain of physical death comes liberation into the life of the spirit. You are more than flesh. You are immortal souls. Once you experience this daily, by learning to temporarily set aside your worldly consciousness, you will be free of the physical plane and death.

"You are a child of the universe. The Light says, 'If you take one step toward me, I will take 10 toward you.' There should be no compulsion in your religion and prayer. Prayer is intended as a joy. It is a song which arises from your heart and lifts you up into the Light. Say the prayer, morning and evening. Open your heart to the possibility you are more than a child of flesh. Try to live a life of service to others. Seek to make each action an opportunity to bring you closer to your higher self and the Light.

"Enlightenment may be attained in every day life. Perfect all your skills; seek personal excellence. Seek to help others. Seek to make each action a prayer to your higher nature and the higher destiny. Then, as the Light wills, you will take your place as a child of the universe.

"Now before I leave, let me give you a present. In the years to come, when you are frightened or lost, say the prayer of submission; focus on the Light and I will be there to help you.

"Now close your eyes. Repeat the prayer and focus on the Light. As you focus on the Light open your right hand and extend it forward."

Then a wondrous thing happened as the people stretched out their hands. The Ancient One slowly turned into a large ball of white, shining Light; and as the Light grew brighter and brighter, slowly, it transformed into a thousand white, glimmering roses. And as the people extended their hands further they accepted the Ancient One's gift. Each held in their hand for a brief moment, a shining, white rose formed by the Light of eternity.

---

It was said each of those present who received the roses of Light were changed. They left the mountain aglow spreading a message of Light, love and hope to the people of the city-plain and countryside. Each in their own way reached completion serving others all the days of their lives.

From this event the Legend spread and the Ancient One's message continues to live. When you are lost or in despair open your hand and heart to the Light. Say the prayer of submission and as the Light wills your problems will turn into solutions.

Extend your hand. Accept what is offered. You too can become a fully conscious child of the universe, living a life of service, love and Light.

———————————•►◆◄•———————————

# Appendix:

# The Sufi Call, Making the World Better

*Nasrudin was now an old man looking back on his life. He sat with his friends in the tea shop telling his story.*

*"When I was young I was firey — I wanted to awaken everyone. I prayed to Allah to give me the strength to change the world.*

*In mid-life I awoke one day and realized my life was half over and I had changed no one so I prayed to Allah to give me the strength to change those around me who so much needed it.*

*Alas, now I am old and my prayer is simpler. 'Allah,' I ask, 'please give me the strength to at least change myself.'"\*\**

# Introduction

According to Sufi tradition, man/woman is the meeting point between heaven and earth and is created with a spiritual destiny. Within each person there is the capacity to create, make decisions and destroy. These aspects or abilities reflect Higher attributes and man/woman's birth right is to rule a vast, personal spiritual kingdom.

Humanity is evolving to a higher state of consciousness. This is both individual and collective- as a race of people. This evolution is purposeful and guided so it may be attained. To help safeguard this Plan there is a hierarchy of servants and teachers who work on many levels. Collectively humanity has a potential and destiny. Many of the holy books speak about this potential. These references are part allegorical and part literal.

In the Plan, each person or soul has a distinctive role. In part, that is what this life is about. To figure out how you fit into the world, using your physical, mental, and spiritual potential. The world needs good people who are doing what they can to make things work for themselves and others.

In each day, there are many opportunities to reach higher and fulfill your individual destiny or plan. Simply ask yourself before doing something that you are uncertain about, if this action will bring you closer or further you from your own higher destiny and the Source. Learn to wait for an answer. You can do this. Slowly you will begin to hear your own inner capacity. Follow this inner voice. This inner voice and its wisdom are aligned with the higher destiny of the universe.

This piece is written for those who will come later and those who might wonder how to make this world a little better. This formula (and Plan) has long existed; it is simple to describe, but O so complex to in act.

# The Formula

First, work on yourself to become the best version of yourself. Second, join hands with others and contribute to making your family, community and world better. In each thought/action reach higher; seek to take the high road: expressing the highest part of self.

# The Inner Journey

The inner journey begins by realizing the potential within and the potential within us all, collectively. Within each there is an empty space that we seek to fill with all kinds of things, people and pursuits. This primal emptiness is part of the reason we came to this planet/realm. We came here to fully express ourselves both as spiritual and physical beings; this emptiness serves as a friction which pushes us forward always searching for that missing piece; wanting more and pushing ourselves to go further. Without it, we would be more or less content with our circumstance and rarely seek to travel further. It is the fire in our belly to go and do, seek and become.

# Filling the Empty Place

Ultimately, this empty place is to be filled with The Light of Eternity; once this missing piece has been identified and added to the mix: higher learning and more purposeful living might begin. You see, in a sense, we were born incomplete so the Light might fill this empty place with spiritual energy and more fully incorporate our other talents; and we have what is termed- *The Completed Person*.

One of the characteristics of this individual, who has reached spiritual completion, is that they are equally concerned about themselves as they are about others. Realizing that if people are to reach their full potential they must be given opportunity to go and become; also realizing that if their brother is hungry, they in a sense are hungry as well. For you see, having experienced the interconnectedness of all living things through the Light, they realize the Higher Potential can only be accomplished if people focus and work together.

94

# Helping Others

The world is a mess right now, because people are not working together to help each other. There are too many takers; key individuals are overly concerned for themselves and are not considering their brothers/sisters at the level necessary. This is the situation where some self-interest is necessary to healthy living but over concern leads to selfishness: which is harmful to self and others.

The first step in making the world better: is to work on yourself; to become the best person that you are capable of becoming. Find out who you are, what talents you have and how they might be incorporated into the world. Each of us has come here with a skill set that will help us fulfill our life plan. This life plan is designed so that you can reach personal excellence and in the process make the world a better place. Better individuals working together help create better outcomes.

Each of us has an individual spiritual destiny and humanity has a collective destiny as well. Through the Light, the entire universe is evolving upward, returning to the place of Origin. When the souls were created they were sent out into the universe with a cosmic mission; to go and create, returning one day more complete in understanding and increased capacity to be One with The Creative Element.

In the earth phase, because of the contrast between the spiritual and physical, greater opportunity exists to create and join with the Creative Element. Within each soul there is an aspect that is most like this Creative Element; it is this aspect which will lead us home through the many worlds and is our compass through the dark night.

# Compromise & the Lower Soul

One of the characteristics of the lower self is that it wants what it wants and reluctantly compromises. Yet, compromise is an essential aspect to living in a family and community; yet it is something which is difficult for the lower soul to learn and accept. Hence, for most there is an ongoing friction between what we want and what the situation may demand.

We see this trait in young children particularly when they are focused on doing something: they will scream and shout- yell and cry, 'I want it now.'

While the response from an adult may be a little more subtle; still the intent is often the same: wanting things their way. The desire to control is a very ancient part of us, and talks to our need for survival and directing our destiny.

Sometimes, this need to have our own way stands in the way of our living harmoniously with others; also it can be an impediment to accepting solutions to complex problems. Sometimes, we have to give-in a little and accept outcomes that we don't want to accept. Remember a compromise is a way of settling differences, by everyone making some concession and often meeting halfway. It implies giving in a little and this is something which is very, very difficult for the untrained lower soul to do; the lower soul wants to be in charge dictating outcomes.

One of the biggest learning experiences for me was the advent of having children. I had to learn to give-up my time and help care for them. While I personally wanted to sleep, my wife and I took turns doing the middle of the night feeding. The lower soul in me was yelling stay in bed, and higher soul was saying, get-up and care for your young one. What made this easier was the love in my heart and it pushed me forward and helped get me out of bed.

Until all people see this dynamic working in themselves and rise above it; the need to get what we want (stay in bed) as opposed to what the situation requires (feed the babe); there will be friction and lack of harmony.

# Caring For My Neighbor

Why should I care about my neighbor? There are many reasons to do so. First nobody lives in isolation; we are social creatures who depend upon each other for our survival and quality of life. Second, if my neighbor is hungry and sick; at some point, these troubling conditions will affect me directly. I may catch whatever disease is affecting my neighbor and eventually no matter his restraint, one day if he continues to stay hungry, he will knock on my door demanding food. We see this throughout history; eventually, oppressed people turn against their oppressors and take back whatever is rightfully theirs. This is a vicious cycle and our best chance for co-existence is mutual sharing of resources.

# Conclusion

Within our universe, there is a primal energy that is life giving, loving and all knowing. This energy is the enabling factor and in time the individual learns to embrace and use this primordial element. Having a part of this element within, slowly the individual recognizes this energy as the Source of their inner burning.

In the journey to completion, each is the prodigal son who returns, with spiritual capacity and is embraced by their Father/Mother to share in the kingdom and their birth right.

Then, gradually as intended, the world becomes a better place: one person at a time.

———————————————

** Posted on **facebook**, by Eric Twose, *The Caravanserai Page*, 7/1/16, 9:51 am.

# OTHER BOOKS BY STEWART BITKOFF

---

- *Journey of Light: Trilogy*
  Authorhouse, 2004.

- *A Commuter's Guide to Enlightenment*
  Llewellyn, 2008.

- *Sufism for Western Seekers*
  Abandoned Ladder, 2011.

- *The Ferryman's Dream*
  Abandoned Ladder, 2012.

- *Beyond The River's Gate*
  Abandoned Ladder, 2014.

- *The Appleseed Journal*
  Abandoned Ladder, 2014.

Books are available on **Amazon.com** in paperback and Kindle version.

# ABOUT THE AUTHOR

Stewart Bitkoff grew up in New York City and spent most of his professional career living and working in the New York City area. An expert in therapeutic recreation and psychiatric rehabilitation and treatment, Dr. Bitkoff has been on the faculty or served as field instructor for multiple colleges and universities.

He has written work centering on the topic of the completed person and the original human development system. For years Dr. Bitkoff studied in two modern mystical schools. Professionally he worked to help the mentally ill integrate their altered states of consciousness into the physical world; recently he worked with children and their families as a behavioral consultant.

Please visit his website at

http://www.stewartbitkoff.com/

or visit on **facebook.**

9 780991 577521